IT'S WOOD

Wood comes from trees, which are grown in many parts of the world. They are cut into logs, which can then be used in many different ways. A lot of wood is used for buildings and furniture because it is strong and long-lasting. It can be burned to give us light and heat. Wood floats on water, so we can use it to build boats. It can be carved into different shapes to make musical instruments or ornaments. Wood is also used to make paper: the pages in this book are made from trees. Look around you and use this book to help you find other things that are made from wood.

There are many kinds of trees in the forest. Each has its own special leaf shape and **bark** pattern.

Look at the rings of wood inside this **trunk**. Trees grow a new ring every year.

KAY DAVI...

...A... It'... W...RLD

A MATERIAL WORLD

It's Glass   It's Plastic
It's Metal   It's Wood

Editor: Joanna Housley
Designer: Loraine Hayes

First published in 1992 by Wayland (Publishers) Ltd

This edition published in 2006 by Wayland, an imprint of Hachette Children's Books

® Copyright 1992 Wayland

British Library Cataloguing in Publication Data
Davies, Kay
It's Wood. – (Material World Series)
I. Title II. Oldfield, Wendy III. Series
620.12

ISBN-10: 0750248521
ISBN-13: 9780750248525

Typeset by Kalligraphic Design Ltd, Horley, Surrey
Printed in China

Hachette Children's Books
338 Euston Road, London NW1 3BH

Words that appear in **bold** in the text are
explained in the glossary on page 22.

When trees have been cut into **logs** they are piled high to dry. They will be sawn into **planks** and **beams**, ready for use.

The wooden beams in this old building were cut and shaped with hand-tools.

The beams are very strong and make the building look attractive.

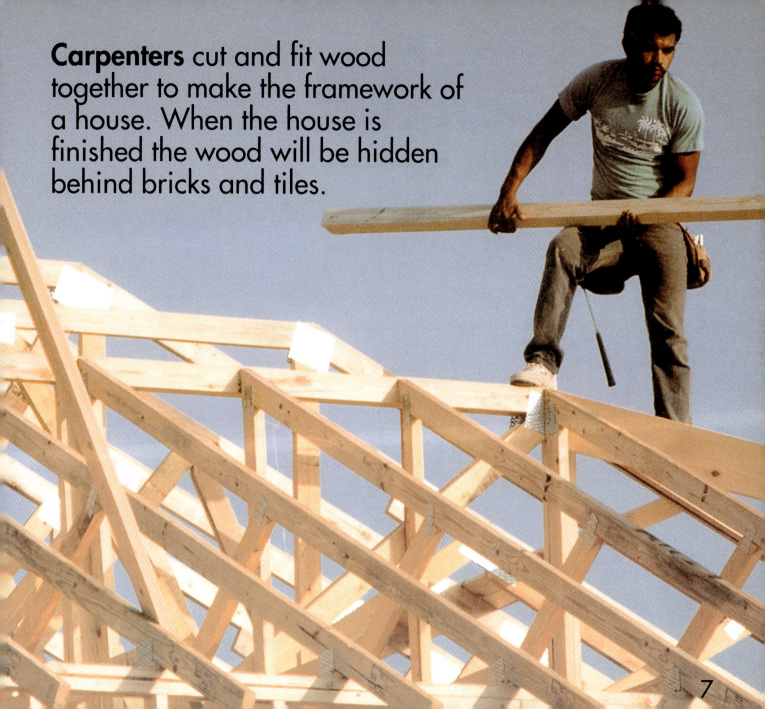

Carpenters cut and fit wood together to make the framework of a house. When the house is finished the wood will be hidden behind bricks and tiles.

The woodpecker taps holes in a tree with its strong beak. It digs out the wood to find insects to eat.

We need tools like this **drill** to make holes in wood.

Tables, chairs and shelves are useful in our homes. We can choose different coloured woods to match our rooms. Look around your home for furniture made from wood.

Wood can be used as a fuel. When it is burnt it gives light and heat. The flames from this log fire make a flickering picture.

Wooden tools and bowls are light and easy to use in the kitchen. The wooden spoon does not absorb heat, so it will not burn our hands.

Thin strips of wood will bend. We can weave baskets of all shapes and sizes from the wood.

Even large planks of wood can be bent when they are wet. They can be shaped to make a boat that will float.

Hockey is fun to play and watch. Players hit the ball with a long wooden stick with a curve at the end. What other games can you play with wood?

We can **carve** wood to make ornaments and decorations for our homes.

These creatures have all been carved from wood. What animals can you see?

The pieces of a jigsaw fit together perfectly. These children are matching the bits of the picture on the pieces of wood to solve the puzzle.

These puppets move when their strings are pulled. Their wooden pieces fit together to move like the bones in our bodies.

The **guitar** has a hollow wooden body. When the strings are plucked, they make a musical sound. Many musical instruments are made of wood. Do you know their names?

Polished wood shines in the light. Necklaces can be made by stringing wooden beads together. Beads and bangles are fun to wear.

Do you like to read books? The paper pages in books are made from **pulped** wood.

What else is paper used for?

We often throw paper away. But it can be collected, cleaned and made into new paper and card. This helps save trees.

GLOSSARY

Bark The outside layer of a tree trunk.

Beams Thick, shaped lengths of wood.

Carpenter A person who cuts and fits wood together.

Carve To cut shapes from wood.

Drill A tool for making holes.

Guitar A musical instrument with six strings.

Hockey A ball game in which two teams of players try to score goals by hitting a ball with long wooden sticks.

Logs Thick wooden pieces cut from trees.

Planks Flat lengths of wood used for building.

Pulped Made wet and soggy.

Trunk The main stem of a tree.

BOOKS TO READ

Ways into Science: Materials/Changing Materials by Peter Riley (Franklin Watts, 2001)

Working with Materials: Joining Materials/ Changing Materials/ Shaping Materials/ Mixing and Separating Materials by Chris Oxlade (Wayland, 2006)

TOPIC WEB

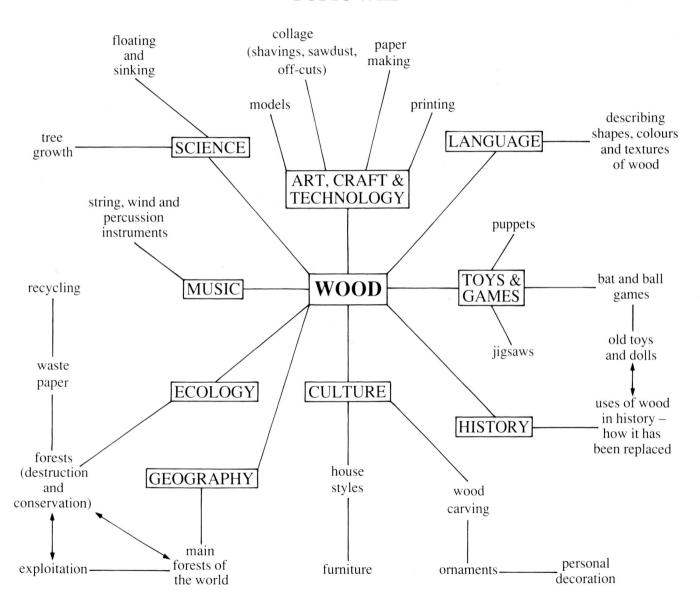

INDEX

Picture acknowledgements

Chapel Studios 4 (inset), 5, 6, 11, 17, 19; Eye Ubiquitous 8 (inset), 13 (Dave Fobister), 15; Skjold 20; Tony Stone Worldwide 8 (main pic); Topham 16; ZEFA 4 (main pic), 7, 9, 10, 18, 21.